MUSICAL INSTRUMENTS

Banjos

RUTH DALY

AV2

www.av2books.com

AV2

Step 1
Go to **www.av2books.com**

Step 2
Enter this unique code
VKTGBM9LU

Step 3
Explore your interactive eBook!

AV2 is optimized for use on any device

Your interactive eBook comes with...

Read

Audio
Listen to the entire book read aloud

Videos
Watch informative video clips

Weblinks
Gain additional information for research

Try This!
Complete activities and hands-on experiments

Key Words
Study vocabulary, and complete a matching word activity

Quizzes
Test your knowledge

Slideshows
View images and captions

View new titles and product videos at www.av2books.com

Banjos Contents

Strum, strum. Pick the strings, too. Playing the banjo is fast and fun!

The banjo is a string instrument. It has a long neck and a round body. Its body is called the pot.

Banjos have four, five, or six strings.

Banjo players strum the strings with their fingers. The strings make sounds when they move. A banjo makes high sounds.

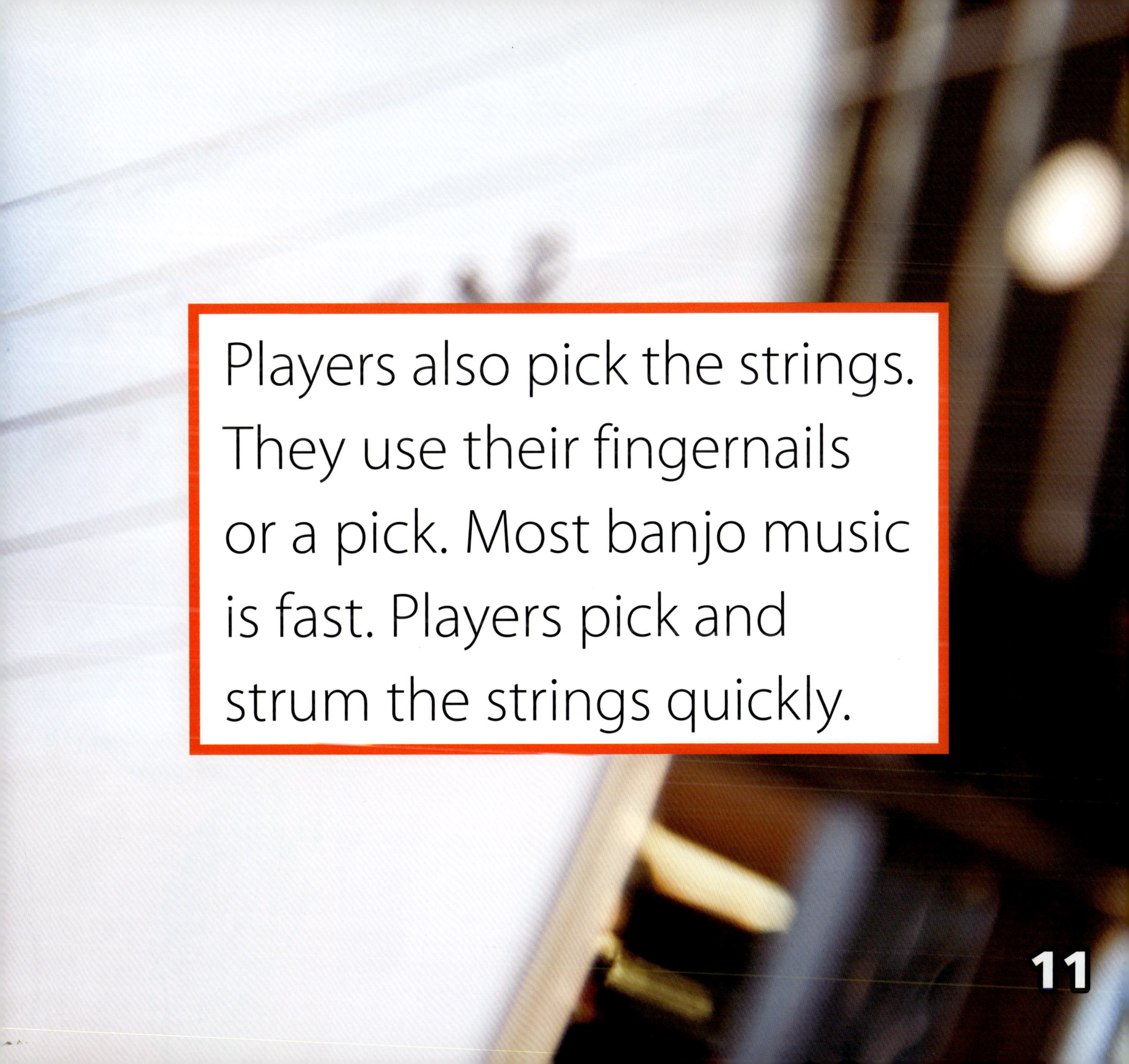

Players also pick the strings. They use their fingernails or a pick. Most banjo music is fast. Players pick and strum the strings quickly.

The back of the pot is open on some banjos. This makes a softer sound. Other banjos have closed backs. These banjos are louder.

Gourds and animal skins were used to make the first banjos. Today, banjo bodies are wood and metal. Wood is used for the neck. Banjo strings are made of metal.

An instrument like the banjo was played in Africa long ago. Today, banjos are important in African American music.

The first banjo instruction manual was written more than 150 years ago.

MUSIC
@
THE
HOUSE
FIRST
DAYS

People sometimes sing funny songs when they play the banjo. They often tell jokes, too.

Earl Scruggs was a popular banjo player. He first played the banjo when he was four years old.

Banjos are popular in bluegrass music. Jazz and folk music also use banjos. Banjos are often played in country music, too.

See what you have learned about banjos.

Which of these pictures does not show a banjo?

KEY WORDS

Research has shown that as much as 65 percent of all written material published in English is made up of 300 words. These 300 words cannot be taught using pictures or learned by sounding them out. They must be recognized by sight. This book contains 56 common sight words to help young readers improve their reading fluency and comprehension. This book also teaches young readers several important content words, such as proper nouns. These words are paired with pictures to aid in learning and improve understanding.

Page	Sight Words First Appearance
5	and, is, the, too
6	a, four, has, have, it, its, long, or
9	high, make, move, sounds, their, they, when, with
11	also, most, use
12	are, back, of, on, open, other, some, these, this
14	animal, first, for, made, to, were
16	American, an, important, in, like, more, than, was, years
19	he, often, old, people, play, sometimes, songs, tell
21	country

Page	Content Words First Appearance
5	banjo, strings
6	body, neck, pot, string instrument
9	fingers, players
11	fingernails, music, pick
14	gourds, metal, skins, wood
16	Africa, African American, instruction manual
19	Earl Scruggs, jokes
21	bluegrass music, country music, folk music, jazz

Published by AV2
350 5th Avenue, 59th Floor New York, NY 10118
Website: www.av2books.com

Library of Congress Cataloging-in-Publication Data

Names: Daly, Ruth, 1962- author.
Title: Banjos / Ruth Daly.
Description: New York : AV2, 2019. | Series: Musical instruments |
Audience: Ages 6-7 | Audience: Grades K-1 |
Identifiers: LCCN 2019045526 (print) | LCCN 2019045527 (ebook) | ISBN 9781791116286 (library binding) |
ISBN 9781791116293 (paperback) | ISBN 9781791116309 | ISBN 9781791116316
Subjects: LCSH: Banjo--Juvenile literature.

Classification: LCC ML1015.B3 D35 2019 (print) | LCC ML1015.B3 (ebook) | DDC 787.8/819--dc23
LC record available at https://lccn.loc.gov/2019045526
LC ebook record available at https://lccn.loc.gov/2019045527

Printed in Guangzhou, China
1 2 3 4 5 6 7 8 9 0 24 23 22 21 20

022020
100919

Project Coordinator: John Willis Designer: Ana María Vidal

The publisher acknowledges Alamy, Getty Images, iStock, and Shutterstock as the primary image suppliers for this title.

MUSICAL INSTRUMENTS

Tubas

RUTH DALY

AV2

www.av2books.com

AV2

Step 1
Go to **www.av2books.com**

Step 2
Enter this unique code

GPXAJAGL3

Step 3
Explore your interactive eBook!

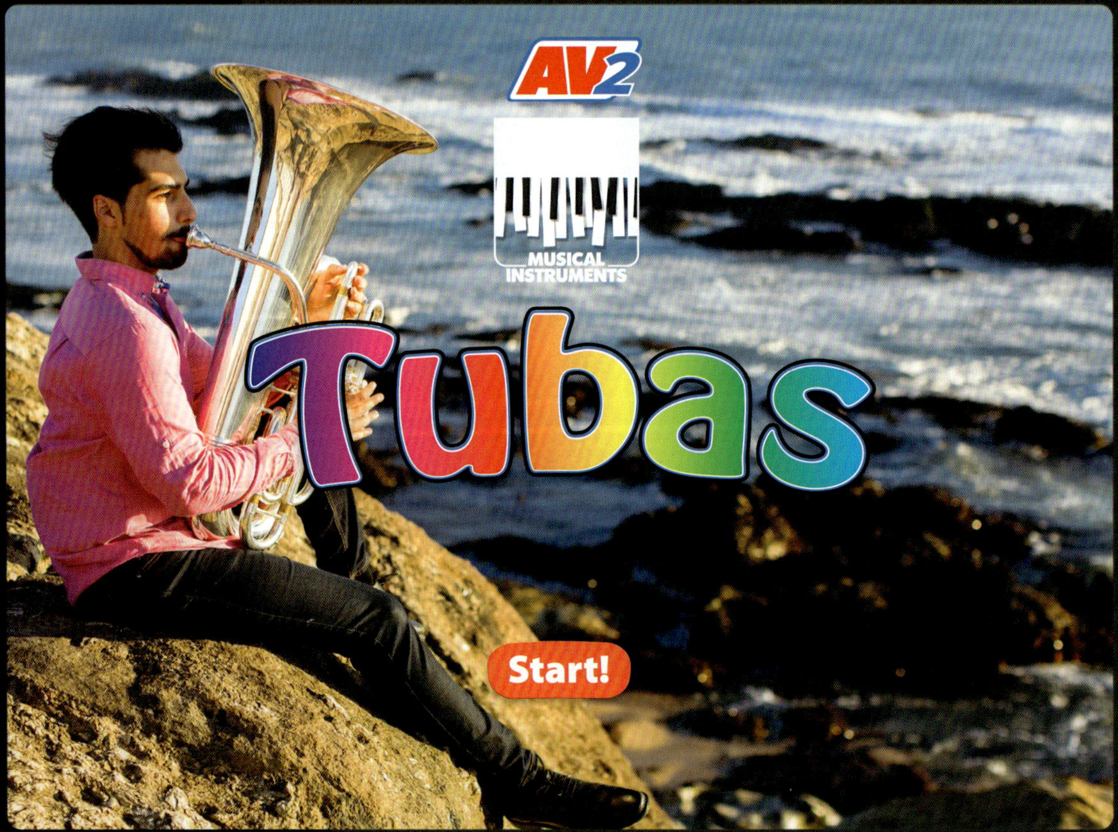

AV2 is optimized for use on any device

Your interactive eBook comes with...

Read

Audio
Listen to the entire book read aloud

Videos
Watch informative video clips

Weblinks
Gain additional information for research

Try This!
Complete activities and hands-on experiments

Key Words
Study vocabulary, and complete a matching word activity

Quizzes
Test your knowledge

Slideshows
View images and captions

View new titles and product videos at www.av2books.com